Feb 19/22

Love Tante Jocelyne
& Uncle Keith

ISBN: 978-1-927042-04-5

Tom's Toy Train

Tom was reading a big blue book. The book was about a toy train. The train came to life. It chugged along and took Tom around the world.

A. Read the story and answer the questions.

1. What colour was the book?

   _____

2. What was the book about?

   _____

3. What came to life?

   _____

4. Where did Tom go?

   _____

ISBN: 978-1-927042-04-5

Phonics: B and T

B. 🖊 **Print B and b on the lines below.**

B

b

C. ✏️ **Colour the pictures that begin with the Bb sound.**

D. 🖊 **Print T and t on the lines below.**

T

t

E. ✏️ **Colour the pictures that begin with the Tt sound.**

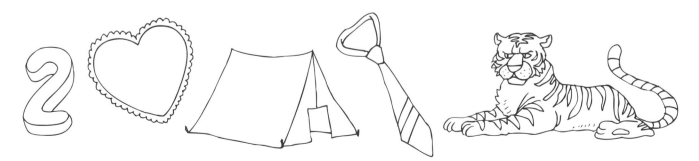

ISBN: 978-1-927042-04-5

 Nouns (1)

- Some **nouns** name people.

F. Underline the nouns that name people.

1. The boy is looking at the train.

2. The story is about a fireman.

3. An animal doctor helps sick animals.

4. A baker makes cookies and cakes.

 **Following Directions**

G. Draw and colour.

1. Draw two toys.
2. Colour the toys.
3. Name the toys.

ISBN: 978-1-927042-04-

Sequencing

The Toy Train

Ted has a toy train. He takes it out of the box. He puts it together. He flips the switch. It goes around the track.

H.   Read the story and the five sentences below. Rewrite them on the lines in the correct order.

It goes around the track.

He puts it together.

Ted has a toy train.

He takes it out of the box.

He flips the switch.

1. _____

2. _____

3. _____

4. _____

5. _____

ISBN: 978-1-927042-04-5

School is starting soon. Today, my mom and I are going to shop for new clothes for school. I want to buy new socks, slacks, and shoes. As a treat, maybe we will have lunch at a restaurant. Shopping for school is fun.

Shopping Fun

A. Read the story and answer the questions.

1. What is starting soon?

   _____

2. When are they going to shop?

   _____

3. What are they shopping for?

   _____

4. What is the treat?

   _____

ISBN: 978-1-927042-04-5

Phonics: C and S

B. 🖊 **Print C and c on the lines below.**

C

c

C. 🖊 **Print the letter C under each picture that begins with the Cc sound.**

D. 🖊 **Print S and s on the lines below.**

S

s

E. ✏ **Colour the pictures that begin with the Ss sound.**

ISBN: 978-1-927042-04-5

 **Nouns (2)**

- *Some **nouns** name places.*

F.   Underline the nouns that name places.

1.   Let's go shopping at the new mall.

2.   We will go to the store after lunch.

3.   The whales live in the ocean.

4.   Last summer, we went to the zoo.

5.   The park has swings.

6.   We visited a farm on our vacation.

 **Following Directions**

G.   Draw and colour.

1.   Draw a big pumpkin.
2.   Colour the pumpkin orange.
3.   Draw yourself in your favourite Halloween costume beside the pumpkin.

 ISBN: 978-1-927042-04-5

Sequencing

H. Look at the pictures. Rewrite the sentences in the correct order.

Baking a Cake

We mix the ingredients.
We put the cake in the oven.
We buy the ingredients.
We spread the icing. Yum! Yum!

1. _____

2. _____

3. _____

4. _____

ISBN: 978-1-927042-04-5

Muffy the New Dog

We have a new dog. His name is Muffy. He has a fluffy grey coat. He likes to play fetch. He sleeps on a carpet beside my bed. I love my new pet.

A. **Read the story. In each sentence, circle ◯ the word that fits best.**

1. Our new pet is a   cat   dog   turtle .

2. Our pet's name is   Fluffy   Puffy   Muffy .

3. Our pet likes to play   catch   fetch   match .

4. Our pet sleeps on a   carpet   blanket   bed .

 Phonics: D and M

B. ✏️ **Print D and d on the lines below.**

D

d

ISBN: 978-1-927042-04-

C. Print M and m on the lines below.

M

m

D. Circle ◯ the correct beginning sound for each picture.

1

d   m

2
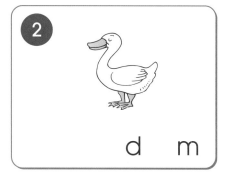
d   m

3

d   m

4
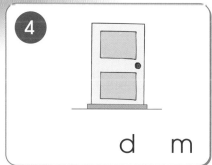
d   m

5
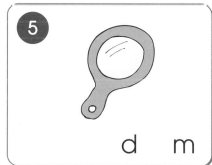
d   m

6

d   m

7

d   m

8

d   m

9
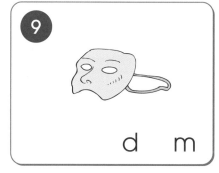
d   m

10
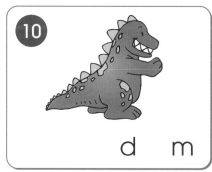
d   m

11

d   m

12

d   m

ISBN: 978-1-927042-04-5

Nouns (3)

- Some nouns name one person or thing. These are **singular nouns**.
- Some nouns name more than one person or thing. These are **plural nouns**.

E. Circle ◯ the words that best describe the picture.

1.	boy	boys	2.	girl	girls
3.	bird	birds	4.	dog	dogs
5.	tree	trees	6.	flower	flowers
7.	swing	swings	8.	squirrel	squirrels

ISBN: 978-1-927042-04-

Sequencing

F.   Look at the pictures. Rewrite the sentences in the correct order.

Moving Day

The movers carried everything onto the truck.

The moving truck came to our house.

The house is empty. Goodbye, house!

The moving truck drove away.

1. _____

2. _____

3. _____

4. _____

ISBN: 978-1-927042-04-5

The Race

Dan and Fiona ran a race. They started at the red line beside the fence. First, Fiona was in front. Then, Dan caught up with her. He ran past her. Finally, Fiona sped past Dan and won the race!

A. Read the story and answer the questions.

1. Who ran in the race?

   _____

2. Where did they start?

   _____

3. Who was in the lead at first?

   _____

4. Who won the race?

   _____

ISBN: 978-1-927042-04-5

Phonics: F and R

B. ✏️ **Print F and f on the lines below.**

F

f

C. ✏️ **Colour the pictures that begin with the Ff sound.**

D. ✏️ **Print R and r on the lines below.**

R

r

E. Draw three things that begin with the Rr sound.

ISBN: 978-1-927042-04-5

Nouns (4)

- Many **plural nouns** are formed by adding "s" to the **singular nouns**.
- Some are formed by adding "es".

F.   For each case, add an "s" or "es" to make more than one.

1.   crayon + s   =

2.   box   + es =

3.   marker + s   =

4.   block   + s   =

5.    dish   + es =

6.    rug   + s   =

Cloze

G.   The pictures tell about the missing words. Put in the words to fit the pictures.

❶    ❷    ❸

1. Roy climbed the _____ to chase the butterfly.

2. The fish swam down the _____ .

3. The _____ burned brightly in the camp.

ISBN: 978-1-927042-04

Following Directions

H. A map helps you find your way around. Look at the map. Draw and colour on the map.

1. Draw a house <u>south</u> of the school.

2. Colour the house red.

3. Draw a car on the street that is <u>east</u> of the person.

4. Draw three trees <u>north</u> of the school.

5. Colour the leaves green and the trunks brown.

6. Draw a swimming pool <u>west</u> of the park.

7. Colour the swimming pool blue.

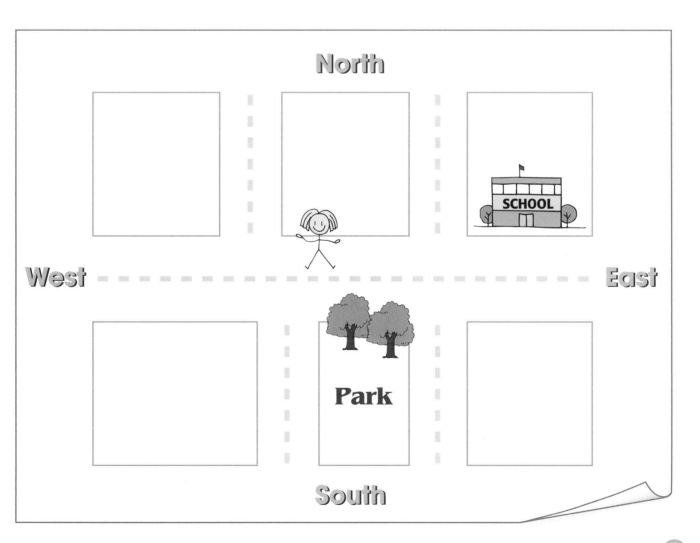

ISBN: 978-1-927042-04-5

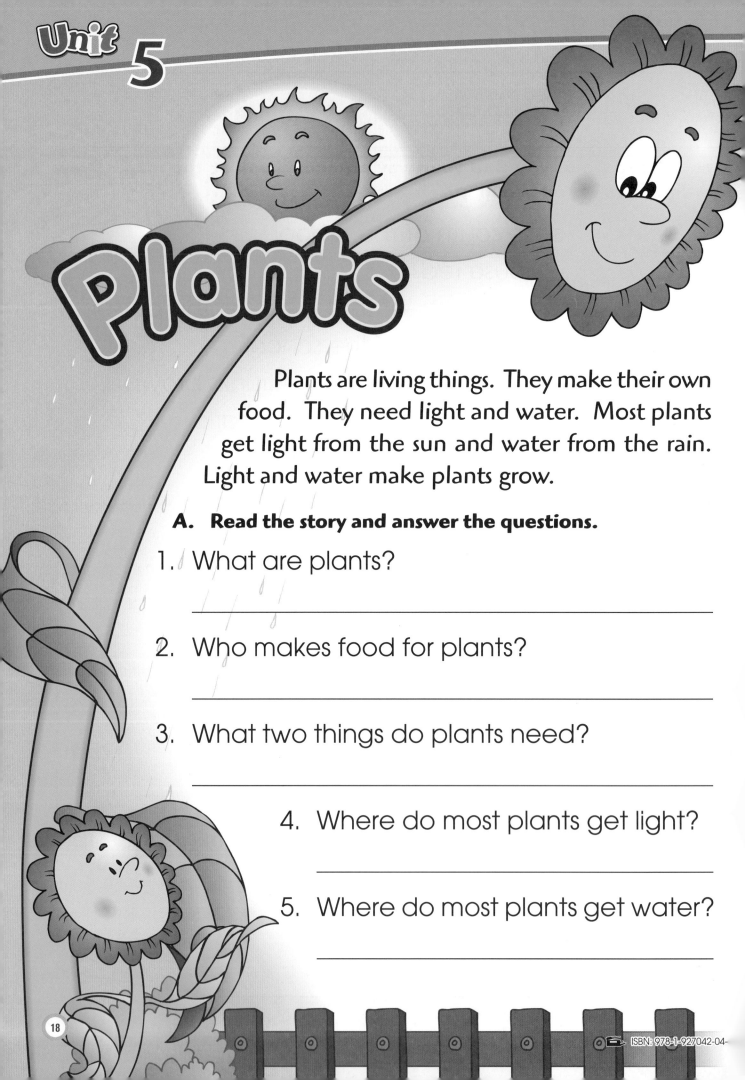

Plants

Plants are living things. They make their own food. They need light and water. Most plants get light from the sun and water from the rain. Light and water make plants grow.

A.   Read the story and answer the questions.

1. What are plants?

_____

2. Who makes food for plants?

_____

3. What two things do plants need?

_____

4. Where do most plants get light?

_____

5. Where do most plants get water?

_____

ISBN: 978-1-927042-04-

Phonics: G and P

B. Print G and g on the lines below.

G

g

C. Print the letter g under each picture that begins with the Gg sound.

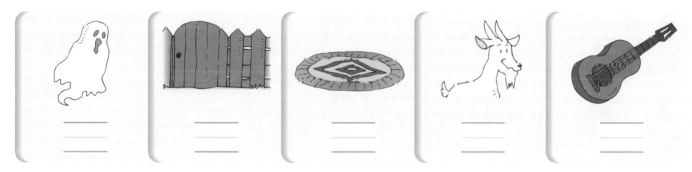

D. Print P and p on the lines below.

P

p

E. Colour the pictures in the pizza slices that begin with the Pp sound.

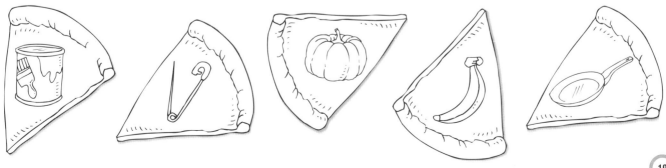

ISBN: 978-1-927042-04-5

 Sentences (1)

- A **sentence** begins with a capital letter and ends with a period.

F. Rewrite the following as sentences.

1. we have a pet cat

_____

2. the apple is tasty

_____

3. it is sunny outside

_____

4. there are rows and rows of corn

_____

Word Puzzles

G. Read the hints and write the words.

1. You can see it in the sky on a bright day.

2. It falls from the sky.

3. This is what you eat.

4. This is what you drink.

5. They are green living things that grow in the soil.

ISBN: 978-1-927042-04-

Sequencing

H. Look at the pictures. Rewrite the sentences in the correct order.

We dig the soil.
The plant sprouts.
It rains; then the sun shines.
We buy the seeds.
We plant the seeds.

1. _____

2. _____

3. _____

4. _____

5. _____

ISBN: 978-1-927042-04-5

Hens and Chicks

Dear Ned,

How are you? I have been learning all about chicks and hens. Did you know that chickens are birds? Hens lay eggs and sit on them to warm them. A baby chick grows inside the egg. Then the chick pecks at the shell when it is ready to hatch. Pop! A new baby chick is born.

Your friend,
Harry

A. Read the letter and answer the questions.

1. What has Harry been learning about?

   _____

2. What kind of animal is a chicken?

   _____

3. Where do baby chicks grow before they hatch?

   _____

4. How do baby chicks hatch?

   _____

ISBN: 978-1-927042-04-5

Phonics: H and N

B. ✏️ **Print H and h on the lines below.**

C. 🖍️ **Colour the pictures that begin with the Hh sound.**

D. ✏️ **Print N and n on the lines below.**

E. **Circle ◯ the correct beginning sound for each picture.**

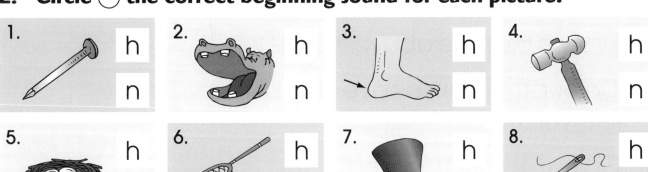

1. h n	2. h n	3. h n	4. h n
5. h n	6. h n	7. h n	8. h n

ISBN: 978-1-927042-04-5

Sentences (2)

- A **sentence** is a group of words. It tells a complete thought about someone or something.
  Example: The flower is pretty.
  (This tells something about the flower.)

F. Write "yes" for sentences. Write "no" for the rest.

1. the baby chick _____

2. Carrots taste good. _____

3. A dog barks. _____

4. man on the moon _____

5. The train chugged along. _____

 Following Directions

G. Read the sentences. Draw and colour the Easter egg.

1. Draw a red line near the bottom of the egg.

2. Draw five circles above the red line. Colour them green.

3. Draw a blue line above the circles.

4. Colour the part above the blue line yellow.

5. Colour the rest of the egg your favourite colour.

ISBN: 978-1-927042-04-5

 **Spelling**

H. Circle ◯ the correct word in each row.

1. chicken   cicken   chickn   chiccken

2. htch   hatch   haetch   heatch

3. pecks   pcks   peks   peacks

 **Sequencing**

I. Look at the pictures. Rewrite the sentences in the correct order.

The baby chick pecks at the shell.
The chick hatches from the egg.
The hen lays an egg.
The hen sits on the egg to warm it.

1. _____

2. _____

3. _____

4. _____

ISBN: 978-1-927042-04-5

Judy the Witch

Judy is a friendly witch. She wears a pair of red magic jumping boots. She likes to jump over trees and houses. When Judy jumps, people watch. She wishes she could jump over the moon, but her jumping boots won't go that high.

A. Read the story. Circle ◯ the correct answers.

1. Judy is a witch. She is _____ .
   mean   fearless   friendly

2. Judy wears magic _____ .
   shoes   hats   boots

3. People _____ when Judy jumps.
   wait   watch   wish

4. Judy wishes she could jump over the _____ .
   trees   moon   houses

ISBN: 978-1-927042-04-

Phonics: J and W

B. Print J and j on the lines below.

J

j

C. Colour the pictures that begin with the Jj sound.

D. Print W and w on the lines below.

W

w

E. Draw the pictures that begin with the Ww sound inside the web.

27

ISBN: 978-1-927042-04-5

 **Verbs**

- **Verbs** *are action words.*
  Example: Mary <u>plays</u> with her dolls.

F.   Underline the verbs in these sentences.

1. Judy wears jumping boots.

2. David plays the guitar.

3. Kathleen looks at the stars.

4. Rob works at school.

5. Mary cooks her dinner.

6. Dad baked a cake.

7. They walked to the store.

8. The girls jumped over the rope.

9. Christina skates every week.

10. Ryan likes baseball.

ISBN: 978-1-927042-04-5

Following Directions

G. Read the sentences. Follow the directions.

1. Draw a witch in the window on the top floor.

2. Draw one door in the middle of the bottom floor.

3. Draw three Jack O'Lanterns in the windows.

4. Draw four ghosts in the garden.

5. Draw a full moon in the sky.

6. Colour the picture.

ISBN: 978-1-927042-04-5

Flying Kites

Let's go fly a kite, up to the sky so bright.
Let's go fly a kite and send it soaring.

Kites for Sale
boxes, diamonds, dragons, and more...
Prices start at $5.00.

A. Read the sign and answer the questions.

1. What is the sign selling?

_____

2. What shapes are the kites?

_____

3. What is so bright?

_____

4. What is the starting price of the kites?

_____

5. How many times does the word "kite(s)" appear on the sign?

_____

 ISBN: 978-1-927042-04-

Phonics: K and V

B. ✏️ **Print K and k on the lines below.**

K

k

C. Join the dots beside the pictures of the words that begin with the Kk sound.

D. ✏️ **Print V and v on the lines below.**

V

v

E. Circle ◯ the words in the word search.

vine   van   vest   violin   valentine   vase

b	d	u	x	c	o	l	v	m	v	r	s	v	a	v	k	m	v	h
q	c	f	h	i	e	v	a	l	e	n	t	i	n	e	g	i	a	k
t	v	i	o	l	i	n	w	f	s	v	a	n	z	s	t	u	s	s
l	a	i	r	a	i	n	r	r	t	t	b	e	o	f	o	v	e	n

ISBN: 978-1-927042-04-5

Unit 8

Sentences (3)

- A **sentence** tells a complete thought about someone or something. It has a subject and a verb.

  Example: The boy jumps.

  subject ⌐   ⌐ verb

F.   Look at the pictures. Read the sentences. Print the letters of the sentences in the boxes.

A. The pig squeals.

B. There are three balloons.

C. There are lots of vegetables.

D. The goose laid a golden egg.

E. The pizza has pepperoni on it.

F. The mushrooms are colourful.

G. The penguin lives in Antarctica.

H. The goat has a kid.

I.   The bell is ringing.

ISBN: 978-1-927042-04

Sequencing

G. Read the story and the instructions. Rewrite the instructions in the correct order.

Today we made a kite. We bought sticks, paper, glue, and string. I cut the paper into a diamond shape. Next, Val cut the string. Then, Keith cut the sticks. Finally, we glued the sticks to the paper and added the string. Then we flew our kite.

Instructions

Fly the kite.
Buy the sticks, paper, glue, and string.
Glue the sticks and string to the paper.
Cut the paper, string, and sticks.

1. _____

2. _____

3. _____

4. _____

ISBN: 978-1-927042-04-5

Zoey at the Zoo

Hi! My name is Zoey. I am a two-year-old zebra. I live at the zoo with my parents, Lily and Luther. Before I was born, my mom and dad came to the zoo from Africa. We like to lie in the warm sun.

A. Read what Zoey says and answer the questions.

1. What kind of animal is Zoey?

   _____

2. Where does Zoey live?

   _____

3. Who are Zoey's parents?

   _____

4. When did Zoey's parents come to live at the zoo?

   _____

5. What does Zoey like to do?

   _____

ISBN: 978-1-927042-04-

Phonics: L and Z

B. 🖊 **Print L and I on the lines below.**

L

C. 🖊 **Print Z and z on the lines below.**

Z

z

D. 🖍 **Colour the pictures pink if they begin with the Ll sound. Colour the pictures yellow if they begin with the Zz sound.**

ISBN: 978-1-927042-04-5

Rhyming Words

- Words that have the same ending vowel and consonant sound are **rhyming words**.

Boo!

E. Read each word and write a word that rhymes with it.

1. Boo! _____

2. hand _____

3. sad _____   4. seed _____

5. game _____   6. bag _____

7. money _____   8. house _____

9. tree _____   10. man _____

Sentences (4)

- Some sentences **tell** about someone or something. They end with **periods**.
- Some sentences **ask** about someone or something. They end with **question marks**.

F. Colour ⬛T if it is a telling sentence. **Colour** ⬛A if it is an asking sentence.

1. Have you seen the zebra?

2. We have a new teacher.

3. How did he fall?

4. She went to the beach.

5. I like to play hopscotch.

ISBN: 978-1-927042-04-

Following Directions

G. Draw the following zoo animals above their names.

a zebra	**an elephant**	**a lion**

Sequencing

H. Look at the pictures. Rewrite the sentences in the correct order.

Finally, I hang my picture on the wall.
First, I colour my picture.
Next, I glue my picture to the construction paper.
Then, I cut out my picture.

1. _____

2. _____

3. _____

4. _____

ISBN: 978-1-927042-04-5

The Fox and the Queen

A queen came upon a fox in the royal woods. She questioned the fox about its home. The fox was cunning. He questioned the queen about her palace. She answered his questions. Late at night, while the palace slept, the fox crept in and stole a box with all of the crown jewels in it. Poor sad queen!

A. Fill in the blanks with words from the story.

A 1._____ met a 2._____ in the royal 3._____ . The fox 4._____ the 5._____ about her 6._____ . The queen answered his 7._____ . The fox was 8._____ . He crept into the 9._____ . While everyone 10._____ , he stole a 11._____ with a lot of 12._____ in it.

ISBN: 978-1-927042-04-5

Phonics: Q and X

B. 🖊 **Print Q and q on the lines below.**

Q

q

C. 🖊 **Print X and x on the lines below.**

X

X

D. 🖍 **Colour the pictures green if they begin with the Qq sound. Colour the pictures red if they end with the Xx sound.**

ISBN: 978-1-927042-04-5

 **Inflections**

E.   Fill in each blank with the correct word.

1.   A queen _____ upon a fox.
     come, came

2.   David and Beth are good _____ .
     dancer, dancers

3.   Kathleen _____ a lot.
     talks, talking

4.   Her _____ is Mary.
     name, names

5.   She is _____ muffins.
     bake, baking

6.   We _____ to the zoo yesterday.
     go, went

7.   Where will she _____ the race?
     run, ran

8.   The dog _____ at the mail carrier.
     bark, barked

ISBN: 978-1-927042-04-5

Sequencing

F.   Look at the pictures. Rewrite the sentences in the correct order.

Decorating the Christmas Tree

We put presents under the tree.
We put a star at the treetop.
We hang lights around the tree.
We turn on the lights. How beautiful!
We put colourful balls on the tree.

1. _____

2. _____

3. _____

4. _____

5. _____

ISBN: 978-1-927042-04-5

The Wild Yak

The wild yak is a large ox. It lives in a place called Tibet. A yak can grow to be 1.8 metres tall. A wild yak has long black hair. It has long horns on its head. It eats grass.

A. Read the story and answer the questions.

1. What type of animal is a wild yak?

_____

2. Where does the wild yak live?

_____

3. What does the wild yak eat?

_____

4. What colour is its hair?

_____

5. How tall are some yaks?

_____

ISBN: 978-1-927042-04-

Phonics: Y

B. ✏️ **Print Y and y on the lines below.**

C. Draw a line from the Y in the yo-yo to each picture that begins with the Yy sound.

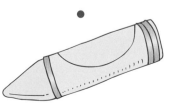

ISBN: 978-1-927042-04-5

Question Words

- Some sentences ask about someone or something. These are **questions**.
- Some questions begin with these words:

  Who   What   Where   When   Why   How

D.   Complete each question with the word that makes sense.

1. _____ can you find the wild yak?   Who   Where

2. _____ is your new teacher?   Why   Who

3. _____ will you go home?   Where   When

4. _____ will you wear today?   How   What

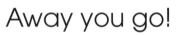 **Sequencing**

E.   Rewrite the sentences in the correct order.

Riding a Bike

Away you go!
Put on a helmet first.
Next, place your feet on the pedals.
Put one leg over the top of the bike to sit down.

1. _____

2. _____

3. _____

4. _____

ISBN: 978-1-927042-04-

Following Directions

F. Read the sentences. Follow the directions.

1. Colour the spaceship your favourite colour.
2. Add a yellow happy face on Dox's T-shirt.
3. Colour Quin's T-shirt orange.
4. Draw Quox next to Quin.
5. Draw another spaceship in the sky.

ISBN: 978-1-927042-04-5

Unit 12

The Tree House

Hello! My name is Robert. In summer, my dad and I built a tree house. We got some wood, some nails, and a hammer. I helped my dad put the tree house together. We built it in the big tree in our backyard. It is fun to play with my friends there.

A. Read the story and answer the questions.

1. What is the name of the boy in the story?

_____

2. What did the boy build with his father?

_____

3. What did they use to build it?

_____

4. Where did they build it?

_____

5. When did they build it?

_____

ISBN: 978-1-927042-04-

Phonics: A, E, I, O, and U

B. Write "a", "e", "i", "o", or "u" in each box. Then read out the words.

1 n ☐ t

2 c l ☐ c k

3 g ☐ f t

4 p ☐ n g u i n

5 l ☐ p s

6 l a d y b ☐ g

7 h ☐ t

8 d ☐ l l

9 ☐ m b r ☐ l l ☐

ISBN: 978-1-927042-04-5

Word Order in Sentences

- *Some **sentences** begin with capital letters and end with periods.*
- *Sentences make sense.*

C. Put the words in the correct order to make sentences. Write the sentences on the lines below.

Example: apple is The juicy.

The apple is juicy.

1. house. a built We tree

_____

2. need yellow I crayon. a

_____

3. cage. bird sings The a in

_____

4. like play to I with dog. my

_____

5. my Look dog. at cute

_____

6. are yummy bananas. They

_____

ISBN: 978-1-927042-04

Following Directions

D. Read the sentences. Follow the directions.

1. Draw a tree and colour the trunk brown.
2. Draw the leaves on the tree. Colour them green.
3. Draw a tree house in the tree.
4. Draw yourself in the picture.
5. Draw the sun in the sky. Colour it yellow.
6. Draw three birds in the sky.

ISBN: 978-1-927042-04-5

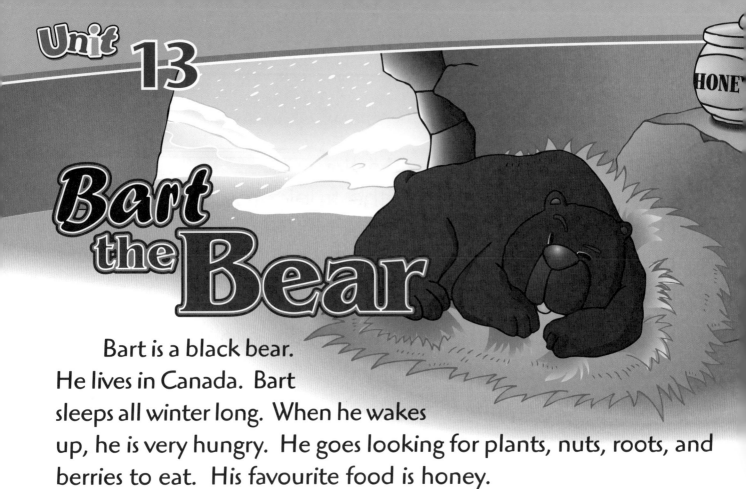

Bart the Bear

Bart is a black bear.
He lives in Canada. Bart
sleeps all winter long. When he wakes
up, he is very hungry. He goes looking for plants, nuts, roots, and
berries to eat. His favourite food is honey.

A. Read the story. Circle ⭕ the correct answers.

1. The story is about a _____ .
   beaver   bear   bird

2. Bart sleeps during _____ .
   summer   day   winter

3. When Bart wakes up, he feels _____ .
   happy   cold   hungry

4. Bart likes to eat _____ .
   roots and berries   apples and oranges

5. _____ is his favourite food.
   Grass   Honey   Hay

6. Black bears live in _____ .
   Canada   Mexico   France

ISBN: 978-1-927042-04

Ending Sounds: B, D, and T

B. Print the letters of the ending sounds.

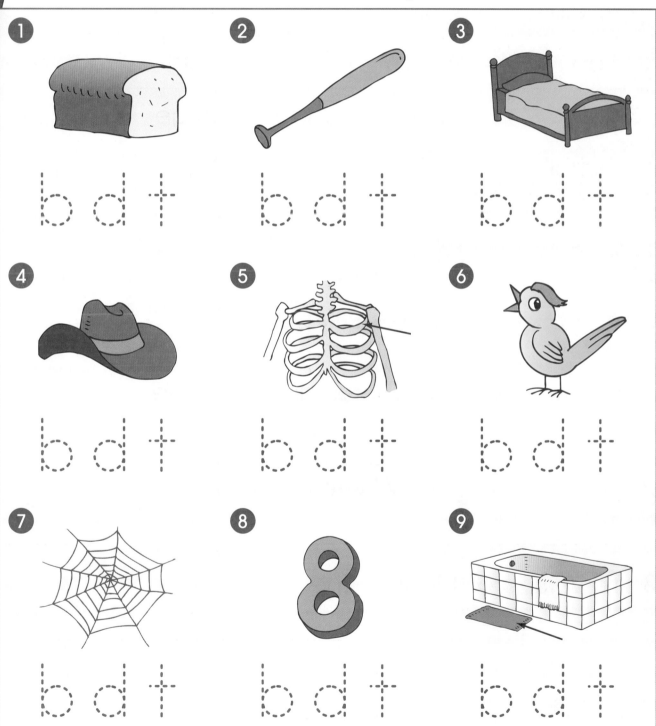

①   b d t

②   b d t

③   b d t

④   b d t

⑤   b d t

⑥   b d t

⑦   b d t

⑧   b d t

⑨   b d t

ISBN: 978-1-927042-04-5

Synonyms

• **Synonyms** are words that have the same meaning.

C. Circle ◯ the synonym for each word on the left.

1. below	in	under	inside	out
2. up	down	out	big	above
3. big	over	under	large	outside
4. small	tiny	big	huge	tall

Word Order in Sentences

D. Put the words in the correct order to make sentences.

1. many bluebirds There are sky. the in

   _____

2. does live? Bart Where

   _____

3. flowers are bloom. The in

   _____

ISBN: 978-1-927042-04-

Sequencing

E. **Look at the pictures. Rewrite the sentences in the correct order.**

I let the yo-yo fall.

My yo-yo goes up and down.

I wind the string around my yo-yo.

I have a yo-yo.

1. _____

2. _____

3. _____

4. _____

ISBN: 978-1-927042-04-5

Making Blueberry Jam

My mom and I are going to make blueberry jam. First, we go to our secret place to pick blueberries from the bushes. Then we sit and pick all the blueberries we want. When we get home, we clean the berries and take out the leaves. Mom puts them in a pot with water and sugar and boils it on the stove. When it is cooled, we taste it. Yum! Yum!

A. Read the story and answer the questions.

1. What is the first thing to do to make blueberry jam?

   _____

2. Where do they go to pick berries?

   _____

3. What do they do after they bring the berries home?

   _____

ISBN: 978-1-927042-04-

Ending Sounds: F, M, and R

B. Colour the pictures in each group that end with the sound of the letter.

ISBN: 978-1-927042-04-5

Tenses

- The **tense** of a verb shows the time of the action.

C. Fill in each blank with the correct word.

1. We   pick, picked   _____ blueberries yesterday.

2. She   is, were   _____ the best dancer here.

3. He   give, gave   _____ them some gum.

4. We   had, has   _____ a good time singing.

5. It   rained, rain   _____ all morning today.

6. She   won, win   _____ the race.

7. Little Jim   want, wanted   _____ to eat the candy.

ISBN: 978-1-927042-04-8

Filling in Speech Bubbles

D. Fill in the words that you think these characters are saying to each other.

 Crossword Puzzle

E. Read the clues and complete the crossword puzzle.

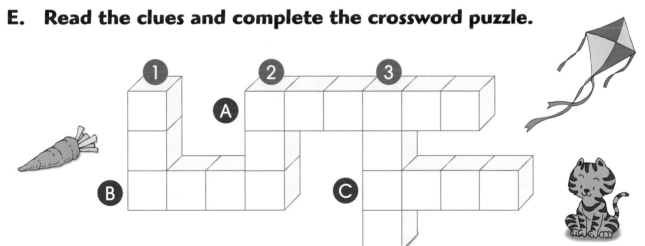

Across

A. what rabbits like to eat

B. place to sleep when camping

C. Let's fly a _____ .

Down

1. flying mammal that hunts at night

2. pet that purrs

3. used to gather fallen leaves

ISBN: 978-1-927042-04-5

Pretty Lights

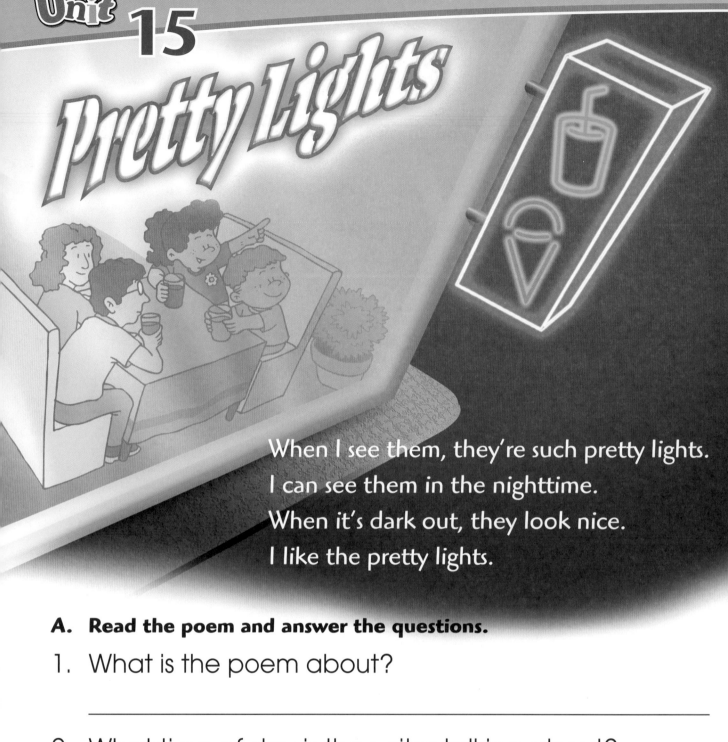

When I see them, they're such pretty lights.
I can see them in the nighttime.
When it's dark out, they look nice.
I like the pretty lights.

A. Read the poem and answer the questions.

1. What is the poem about?

   _____

2. What time of day is the writer talking about?

   _____

3. Do you think the lights are in the country or the city?

   _____

4. Have you ever seen pretty lights? Where?

   _____

ISBN: 978-1-927042-04-5

Ending Sounds: G, K, and S

B. Colour the pictures in each group that end with the sound of the letter.

g

s

Antonyms

- **Antonyms** *are words that are opposites.*

   Examples: hot ⟶ cold

   long ⟶ short

C. Circle ◯ the antonym of the first word in each row.

1.	**day**	night	week	time
2.	**hard**	rough	soft	slimy
3.	**stop**	red	look	go
4.	**white**	blue	green	black
5.	**no**	maybe	was	yes
6.	**happy**	sad	feel	fun
7.	**big**	wide	little	huge
8.	**asleep**	tired	night	awake

ISBN: 978-1-927042-04-5

Word Search

D. **Find these words in the word search. Highlight them with a yellow crayon.**

stop   children   coin   bat   turtle   leaf

castle   tomorrow   light   hop   today   school

B	L	N	P	E	C	A	S	T	L	E	E	S
N	R	R	A	K	V	O	M	U	K	X	N	N
G	F	O	C	H	I	L	D	R	E	N	T	Y
J	U	X	O	M	J	D	E	T	A	U	R	B
S	T	M	I	R	O	T	W	L	I	G	H	T
U	J	F	N	E	C	H	J	E	O	C	L	V
B	S	J	Y	F	L	C	N	S	E	V	O	I
K	T	A	V	C	N	E	D	B	G	H	P	S
T	O	M	O	R	R	O	W	S	C	L	O	D
O	P	B	C	A	C	L	E	V	Y	E	G	E
D	R	L	H	G	O	C	A	C	B	A	T	R
A	U	I	V	D	J	H	F	R	A	F	S	M
Y	N	C	S	C	H	O	O	L	U	E	B	I
V	B	A	F	J	S	P	L	D	T	S	U	A

ISBN: 978-1-927042-04-5

A. Read the sentences in each group. Circle ◯ the correct answer.

1. I am round.
I make a sound.
You use sticks to play me.
What am I?

   a doll   a drum
   a guitar   a ball

2. I am hot.
I look yellow.
I heat the Earth.
What am I?

   the sun   the cloud
   the sky   the moon

3. I am round.
I can bounce.
I can roll.
What am I?

   a ball   a book
   a doll   a flower

4. I am round.
I am made of metal.
You can buy things with me.
What am I?

   a coin   a candle
   a crane   a carrot

5. I can be hard.
I can be soft.
You read me.
What am I?

   a book   a box
   a hook   a doll

ISBN: 978-1-927042-04-

Ending Sounds: L, N, and P

b a l l   f a n    c u p

B. Draw a line from each letter to the picture that ends with the sound of that letter.

 •

 •

 •

 l

 •

 •

 n

 •

 •

 p

 •

 •

 •

ISBN: 978-1-927042-04-5

Rhyming Words

- **Rhyming words** *sound the same at the end.*
  Examples: cat   bat   sat

C.   Circle ◯ the word in each row that rhymes with the first word.

1.	**rug**	cup	mug	hot
2.	**go**	to	gone	so
3.	**fun**	here	run	walk
4.	**tag**	game	it	bag
5.	**red**	bed	stop	blue
6.	**hot**	cold	pot	cat
7.	**sit**	up	at	it
8.	**book**	read	ton	hook
9.	**cake**	eat	bake	ice

ISBN: 978-1-927042-04

Following Directions

D. Read the sentences. Follow the directions.

1. Draw your family.

2. Draw your house.

3. Draw your favourite pet.

4. Draw your favourite T-shirt.

5. Draw your favourite toy.

6. Write your name.

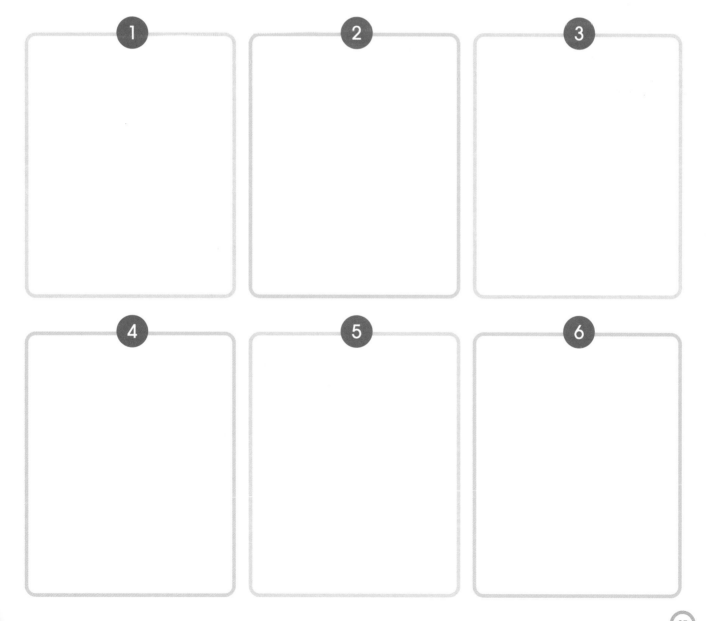

ISBN: 978-1-927042-04-5

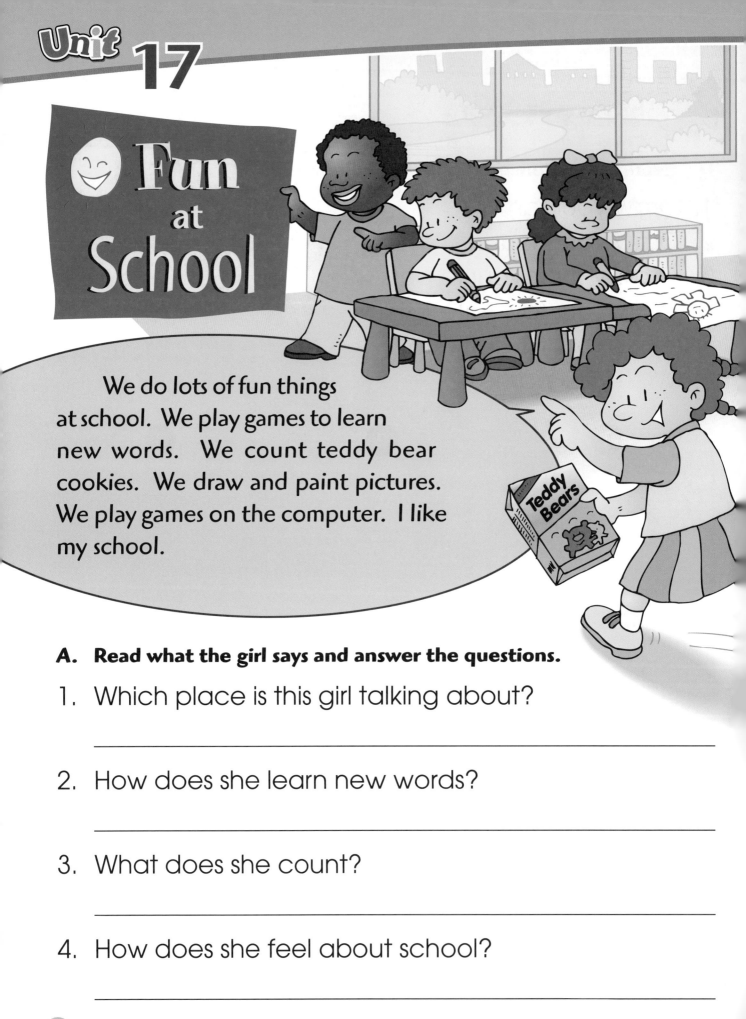

Fun at School

We do lots of fun things at school. We play games to learn new words. We count teddy bear cookies. We draw and paint pictures. We play games on the computer. I like my school.

A. Read what the girl says and answer the questions.

1. Which place is this girl talking about?

   _____

2. How does she learn new words?

   _____

3. What does she count?

   _____

4. How does she feel about school?

   _____

ISBN: 978-1-927042-04

Phonics: Beginning and Ending Sounds

B. Look at the pictures. Fill in the missing letters for each word.

1

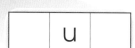

	u	

2

	a	

3

	e	

4

	o	

5

	a	l	

6

	e	n	

7

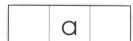

	a	

8

	a	

9

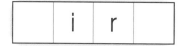

	i	r	

10

	o	o	

11

	a	

12

	a	

ISBN: 978-1-927042-04-5

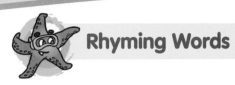 **Rhyming Words**

C. Read the word at the top of each column. Add letters to form words that rhyme with it.

> *They sound the same at the end.*

1. c a t	2. c r i b	3. s a d
☐ a t	☐ i b	☐ a d
☐ a t	☐ i b	☐ a d
☐ a t	☐ i b	☐ a d

4. s i t	5. c a p	6. l i d
☐ i t	☐ a p	☐ i d
☐ i t	☐ a p	☐ i d
☐ i t	☐ a p	☐ i d

ISBN: 978-1-927042-04-

Word Search

D. **Find these words in the word search. Put a line through each word when you find it.**

box   ball   doll   cat   bad   bib
dog   drum   bird   pan   door   bed
cup   hat   cap   top   bag   tent

G	A	B	F	H	B	K	S	N	O	B	M	W
U	T	N	G	D	O	L	L	T	N	A	C	F
D	B	L	H	O	X	A	B	I	R	D	C	M
U	E	O	T	O	U	F	C	U	P	Q	J	Q
V	R	F	U	R	L	P	Q	D	V	W	V	F
X	Y	B	H	T	C	A	P	R	J	B	A	G
T	N	G	D	H	U	N	Q	U	X	I	V	N
R	O	Y	X	A	M	P	C	M	O	B	H	B
S	T	E	N	T	J	Y	N	X	I	T	R	E
E	K	V	R	N	W	B	A	L	L	G	D	D
O	L	X	S	U	F	C	P	E	F	W	O	X
T	O	P	C	A	T	I	G	H	G	T	G	A

ISBN: 978-1-927042-04-5

Sweet Maple Syrup

One sunny morning in March, Sam went on a trip to the Sugar Bush. He saw many tall maple trees. The sap from the trees flowed into buckets. The sap was boiled in a big kettle to make thick, sweet maple syrup. Yum! Yum!

A.   Read the story. Circle ◯ the correct answers.

1. Sam went to the _____ .
    maple garden   Sugar Bush   zoo

2. There were many tall _____ trees.
    pine   maple   apple

3. The sap ran into _____ .
    pockets   baskets   buckets

4. The sap became _____ .
    syrup   sugar   candy

ISBN: 978-1-927042-04-5

Crossword Puzzle

B. **Read the clues and complete the crossword puzzle.**

SWEET   MAPLE

TALL   BUCKETS   THICK

MARCH   SYRUP

Across

A.   the month before April

B.   the opposite of short

C.   It is made from sap.

Down

1.   This taste is good.

2.   pails

3.   the opposite of thin

4.   a kind of tree

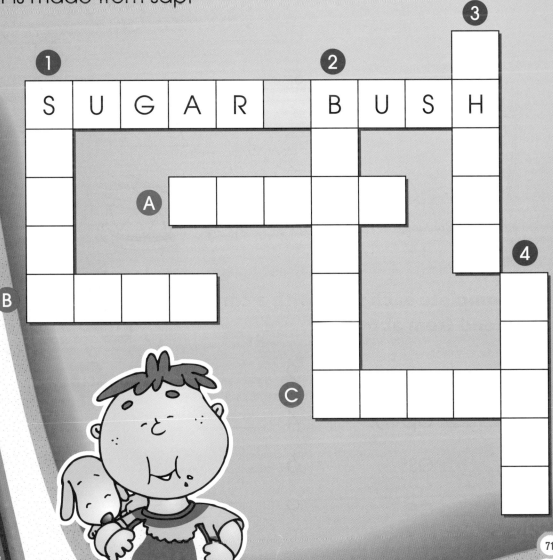

ISBN: 978-1-927042-04-5

Phonics: Consonant Blends

C. Colour the pictures that begin with the given blends.

D. Complete each word with a correct blend from above.

1. __ __ oom

2. __ __ oss

3. __ __ apes

4. __ __ ayon

5. __ __ ass

6. __ __ um

7. __ __ og

8. __ __ ee

9. __ __ ize

10. __ __ own

ISBN: 978-1-927042-04-5

Rhyming Words

E. Draw lines to join the words that rhyme.

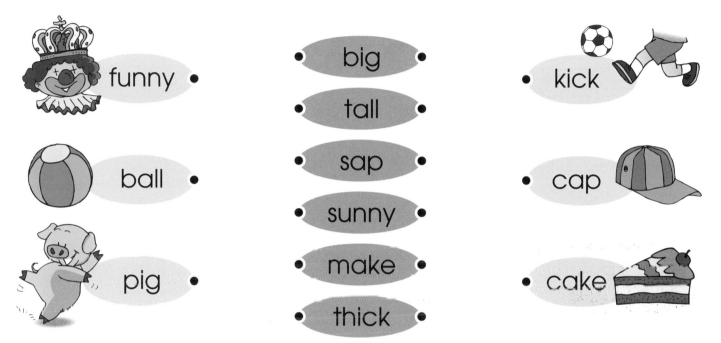

funny

ball

pig

big

tall

sap

sunny

make

thick

kick

cap

cake

Sentences

F. Cross out the sentence that does not belong.

1. My name is Jenny. The children went on a trip. They saw many tall trees.

2. I have pancakes for breakfast. I put maple syrup on the pancakes. The cat is sleeping.

3. We have a maple tree in front of our house. It is tall. Go Leafs go!

4. Pat has one brother and one sister. April is in spring. December is in winter.

ISBN: 978-1-927042-04-5

ISBN: 978-1-927042-04-

1 Tom's Toy Train

A. 1. It was blue.
2. It was about a toy train.
3. The train came to life.
4. He went around the world.

C.

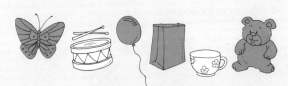

E.

F. 1. The <u>boy</u> is looking at the train.
2. The story is about a <u>fireman</u>.
3. An animal <u>doctor</u> helps sick animals.
4. A <u>baker</u> makes cookies and cakes.

G. (Suggested drawing and answer)

doll   ball

H. 1. Ted has a toy train.
2. He takes it out of the box.
3. He puts it together.
4. He flips the switch.
5. It goes around the track.

2 Shopping Fun

A. 1. School is starting soon.
2. They are going to shop today.
3. They are shopping for new clothes for school.
4. They will have lunch at a restaurant.

C.

E.

F. 1. Let's go shopping at the new <u>mall</u>.
2. We will go to the <u>store</u> after lunch.

3. The whales live in the <u>ocean</u>.
4. Last summer, we went to the <u>zoo</u>.
5. The <u>park</u> has swings.
6. We visited a <u>farm</u> on our vacation.

G. (Suggested drawing)

Draw yourself here.

H. 1. We buy the ingredients.
2. We mix the ingredients.
3. We put the cake in the oven.
4. We spread the icing. Yum! Yum!

3 Muffy the New Dog

A. 1. dog
2. Muffy
3. fetch
4. carpet

D. 1. m   2. d   3. m   4. d
5. m   6. d   7. d   8. m
9. m   10. d   11. m   12. d

E. 1. boy   2. girls
3. birds   4. dog
5. tree   6. flowers
7. swing   8. squirrels

F. 1. The moving truck came to our house.
2. The movers carried everything onto the truck.
3. The moving truck drove away.
4. The house is empty. Goodbye, house!

4 The Race

A. 1. Dan and Fiona ran in the race.
2. They started at the red line beside the fence.
3. Fiona was in the lead at first.
4. Fiona won the race.

C.

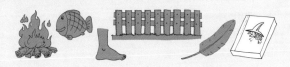

E. (Suggested drawing)

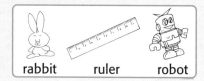

rabbit   ruler   robot

ISBN: 978-1-927042-04-5

Answers

F. 1. crayons   2. boxes
   3. markers   4. blocks
   5. dishes   6. rugs

G. 1. fence   2. river/stream
   3. fire

H.   (Suggested drawing)

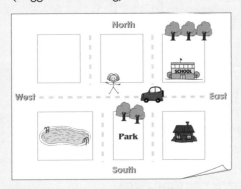

5   Plants

A. 1. Plants are living things.
   2. They make their own food.
   3. They need light and water.
   4. They get light from the sun.
   5. They get water from the rain.

C.

E.

F. 1. We have a pet cat.
   2. The apple is tasty.
   3. It is sunny outside.
   4. There are rows and rows of corn.

G.   (Suggested answers)
   1. sun   2. rain
   3. food   4. water
   5. plants

H. 1. We buy the seeds.
   2. We dig the soil.
   3. We plant the seeds.
   4. It rains; then the sun shines.
   5. The plant sprouts.

6   Hens and Chicks

A. 1. He has been learning about chicks and hens.
   2. It is a bird.
   3. They grow inside eggs.
   4. They peck at the shells.

C.

E.

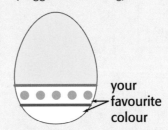

F. 1. no   2. yes
   3. yes   4. no
   5. yes

G.   (Suggested drawing)

your favourite colour

H. 1. chicken   2. hatch
   3. pecks

I. 1. The hen lays an egg.
   2. The hen sits on the egg to warm it.
   3. The baby chick pecks at the shell.
   4. The chick hatches from the egg.

7   Judy the Witch

A. 1. friendly   2. boots
   3. watch   4. moon

C.

ISBN: 978-1-927042-04

E.

F. 1. Judy <u>wears</u> jumping boots.
   2. David <u>plays</u> the guitar.
   3. Kathleen <u>looks</u> at the stars.
   4. Rob <u>works</u> at school.
   5. Mary <u>cooks</u> her dinner.
   6. Dad <u>baked</u> a cake.
   7. They <u>walked</u> to the store.
   8. The girls <u>jumped</u> over the rope.
   9. Christina <u>skates</u> every week.
   10. Ryan <u>likes</u> baseball.

G. (Suggested drawing and individual colouring)

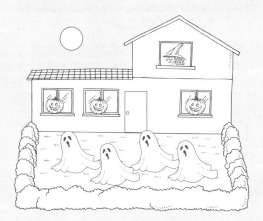

8 Flying Kites

A. 1. It is selling kites.
   2. They are boxes, diamonds, dragons, and more.
   3. The sky is so bright.
   4. It is $5.00.
   5. It appears three times.

C.

E.

b	d	u	x	c	o	l	v	m	v	r	s	v	a	v	k	m	v	h
q	c	f	h	i	e	v	a	l	e	n	t	i	n	e	g	i	a	k
t	v	i	o	l	i	n	w	f	s	v	a	n	z	s	t	u	s	s
l	a	i	r	a	i	n	r	r	t	t	b	e	o	f	o	v	e	n

F. 1. I   2. B
   3. H   4. G
   5. D   6. C
   7. F   8. A
   9. E

G. 1. Buy the sticks, paper, glue, and string.
   2. Cut the paper, string, and sticks.
   3. Glue the sticks and string to the paper.
   4. Fly the kite.

9 Zoey at the Zoo

A. 1. Zoey is a zebra.
   2. Zoey lives at the zoo.
   3. Lily and Luther are Zoey's parents.
   4. They came to live at the zoo before Zoey was born.
   5. Zoey likes to lie in the warm sun.

D.

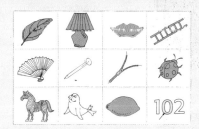

E. (Suggested answers)
   1. zoo   2. sand
   3. bad   4. feed
   5. name   6. tag
   7. honey   8. mouse
   9. free   10. can

F. 1. A   2. T
   3. A   4. T
   5. T

G. (Suggested drawing)

H. 1. First, I colour my picture.
   2. Next, I glue my picture to the construction paper.
   3. Then, I cut out my picture.
   4. Finally, I hang my picture on the wall.

ISBN: 978-1-927042-04-5

Answers

10 The Fox and the Queen

A. 1. queen   2. fox
  3. woods   4. questioned
  5. queen   6. palace
  7. questions   8. cunning
  9. palace   10. slept
  11. box   12. jewels

D.

E. 1. came   2. dancers
  3. talks   4. name
  5. baking   6. went
  7. run   8. barked

F. 1. We hang lights around the tree.
  2. We put colourful balls on the tree.
  3. We put a star at the treetop.
  4. We put presents under the tree.
  5. We turn on the lights. How beautiful!

11 The Wild Yak

A. 1. It is a large ox.
  2. It lives in Tibet.
  3. It eats grass.
  4. Its hair is black.
  5. They are 1.8 metres tall.

C.

D. 1. Where   2. Who
  3. When   4. What

E. 1. Put on a helmet first.
  2. Put one leg over the top of the bike to sit down.
  3. Next, place your feet on the pedals.
  4. Away you go!

F. (Individual colouring and drawing)

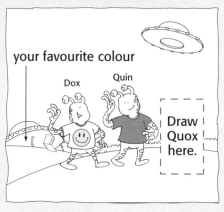

your favourite colour

Dox   Quin

Draw Quox here.

12 The Tree House

A. 1. His name is Robert.
  2. He built a tree house with his father.
  3. They used some wood, some nails, and a hammer to build it.
  4. They built it in the big tree in their backyard.
  5. They built it in summer.

B. 1. e   2. o
  3. i   4. e
  5. i   6. u
  7. a   8. o
  9. u ; e ; a

C. 1. We built a tree house.
  2. I need a yellow crayon.
  3. The bird sings in a cage.
  4. I like to play with my dog.
  5. Look at my cute dog.
  6. They are yummy bananas.

D. (Suggested drawing)

Draw yourself here.

13 Bart the Bear

A. 1. bear   2. winter
  3. hungry   4. roots and berries
  5. Honey   6. Canada

ISBN: 978-1-927042-04-

B. 1. d   2. t
    3. d   4. t
    5. b   6. d
    7. b   8. t
    9. t
C. 1. under   2. above
    3. large   4. tiny
D. 1. There are many bluebirds in the sky.
    2. Where does Bart live?
    3. The flowers are in bloom.
E. 1. I have a yo-yo.
    2. I wind the string around my yo-yo.
    3. I let the yo-yo fall.
    4. My yo-yo goes up and down.

14 Making Blueberry Jam

A. 1. The first thing is to pick blueberries.
    2. They go to their secret place.
    3. They clean the berries and take out the leaves.
B.

C. 1. picked   2. is
    3. gave   4. had
    5. rained   6. won
    7. wanted
D. (Individual writing)
E.

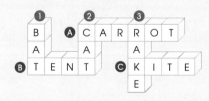

15 Pretty Lights

A. 1. It is about pretty lights.
    2. The writer is talking about nighttime.
    3. They are in the city.
    4. (Individual writing)

B.

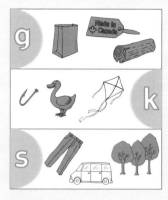

C. 1. night   2. soft
    3. go   4. black
    5. yes   6. sad
    7. little   8. awake
D.

B	I	N	P	F	C	A	S	T	I	F	E	S
N	R	R	A	K	V	O	M	U	K	X	N	N
G	F	O	C	H	I	L	D	R	E	N	T	Y
J	U	X	O	M	J	D	E	T	A	U	R	B
S	I	M	I	R	O	T	W	L	I	G	H	T
U	J	F	N	E	C	H	J	E	O	C	L	V
B	S	J	Y	F	L	C	N	S	E	V	O	I
K	T	A	V	C	N	E	D	B	G	H	P	S
T	O	M	O	R	R	O	W	S	C	L	O	D
O	P	B	C	A	C	L	E	V	Y	E	G	E
D	R	L	H	G	O	C	A	C	B	A	T	R
A	U	I	V	D	J	H	F	R	A	F	S	M
Y	N	C	S	C	H	O	O	L	U	E	B	I
V	B	A	F	J	S	P	L	D	T	S	U	A

16 What Am I?

A. 1. a drum   2. the sun
    3. a ball   4. a coin
    5. a book
B.

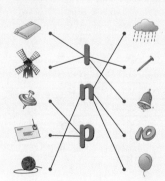

C. 1. mug   2. so
    3. run   4. bag
    5. bed   6. pot
    7. it   8. hook
    9. bake
D. (Individual drawings and answer)

ISBN: 978-1-927042-04-5

17 Fun at School

A. 1. She is talking about her school.
2. She plays games to learn new words.
3. She counts teddy bear cookies.
4. She likes her school.

B. 1. c ; p   2. h ; t
3. b ; d   4. t ; p
5. b ; l   6. t ; t
7. j ; m   8. b ; g
9. b ; d   10. d ; r
11. p ; n   12. c ; t

C. (Suggested answers)
1. bat ; fat ; mat   2. bib ; nib ; rib
3. bad ; dad ; mad   4. fit ; hit ; kit
5. gap ; lap ; map   6. bid ; did ; kid

D.

G	A	B	F	H	B	K	S	N	O	B	M	W
U	T	N	G	D	O	L	L	T	N	A	C	F
D	B	L	H	O	X	A	B	I	R	D	C	M
U	E	O	T	O	U	F	C	U	P	Q	J	Q
V	R	F	U	R	L	P	Q	D	V	W	V	F
X	Y	B	H	T	C	A	P	R	J	B	A	G
T	N	G	D	H	U	N	Q	U	X	I	V	N
R	O	Y	X	A	M	P	C	M	O	B	H	B
S	T	E	N	T	J	Y	N	X	I	T	R	E
E	K	V	R	N	W	B	A	L	L	G	D	D
O	L	X	S	U	F	C	P	E	F	W	O	X
T	O	P	C	A	T	I	G	H	G	T	G	A

C.

D. (Suggested answers)
1. br   2. cr
3. gr   4. cr
5. gr   6. dr
7. fr   8. tr
9. pr   10. cr

E.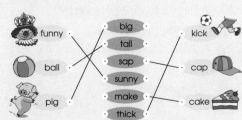

funny   big   kick
  tall
ball   sap   cap
  sunny
pig   make   cake
  thick

F. 1. My name is Jenny.
2. The cat is sleeping.
3. Go Leafs go!
4. Pat has one brother and one sister.

18 Sweet Maple Syrup

A. 1. Sugar Bush   2. maple
3. buckets   4. syrup

B.

ISBN: 978-1-927042-04-